SUSAN SAY

Advent for the whole church community

- All-age Sunday worship in Advent
- Day and night prayers for Advent
- Carol service
- `Away day´ for Advent
- `Open church´ days in Advent
- Making an Advent wreath

kevin mayhew

First published in 2003 by

KEVIN MAYHEW LTD
Buxhall, Stowmarket, Suffolk, IP14 3BW
E-mail: info@kevinmayhewltd.com

KINGSGATE PUBLISHING INC
1000 Pannell Street, Suite G, Columbia, MO 65201
E-mail: sales@kingsgatepublishing.com

9 8 7 6 5 4 3 2 1 0

ISBN 184417 142 6
Catalogue No 1500633

Cover design by Angela Selfe
Edited by Katherine Laidler
Typesetting by Louise Selfe
Printed in Great Britain

Contents

Introduction

For most people Christmas begins in earnest with December and finishes on the 25th of the month, or possibly the 26th if you're really keen.

Where does that pressure place us as a church community? Do we ignore Advent and join the culture we are part of, or do we fight desperately against the incoming tide of Christmas washing menacingly around our Advent sandcastle?

It seems to me that we can join a long and hallowed tradition of recognising what is going on and using it to teach us new truths about the Advent season. A by-product of this is that all the Christmassy December preparations and celebrations can be given a significantly Advent flavour, refreshing them from what for many has become a least favourite and most harassed time of year.

This book is a resource for you to use individually, in household groups at home, in schools and in church.

Scripts and activity instructions are all copiable. Use all the ideas just as they are, or as a starting point for your own planning. Allow them to free you up from the pressure so you can focus on what is really important at this time of year!

Catching the mood of the Advent season

In the season of Advent the whole people of God are waiting, expectant and attentive. We are, collectively, a bit like Elijah making his way through the desert to the holy mountain and standing there on the rock as God shows us the fire and thunder and violent winds but is eventually discovered in the 'still small voice'.

We are a bit like the exiled community taking a straight and honest look at the big questions we cannot ignore, even if they lead us into territory which scares us. We sit around the fireside together, running our memories over the ancient stories and trying to discern in them God's will for us in the present and the future.

We are, collectively, a bit like a woman in pregnancy, aware of growth within us but looking forward to a face-to-face encounter with the life we experience but which is still hidden from our eyes.

'Re-membering' all this puts us together again both as individuals and as God's people. To celebrate Christmas as the coming to birth of a collectively experienced Advent 'gestation' is a completely different experience from celebrating Christmas for a month in advance of Christmas Day. You will find it changes and enriches you as a community, and the festival of Christmas will take on a whole new meaning, clearing away the accumulated rubbish of financial worry, time and energy stress, overwork and exhaustion, and – one of the biggest misunderstandings of all – that Christmas is really a children's festival.

Christmas isn't a children's festival, any more than Good Friday is really for the dying. Such a spin is dangerous, turning the extraordinary touch of the human and divine into little more than a rather pointless spoilt brat zone. No wonder the stress and exhaustion set in – we're getting maximum hassle for minimum return. Perhaps now, more than ever before, we as church need to be faithful at telling the real story of good news. And we will tell that story best by the alternative way we live these weeks of Advent, by the priorities which keep us focused on, and anchored by, God's quiet voice of love.

Having an all-age approach to Advent is not about providing yet more entertainment for the children, but hauling back the runaway season so that it properly belongs to the whole community, with *all* its age groups. Advent invites us – as a whole age-group community

– to explore all those deep questions about life, peering courageously into the darkness together and recognising it as such; watching and waiting together as the light of hope flickers and grows.

So an all-age Advent resource needs to have quite a 'grown-up' feel to it – and even young children do actually want to be full members of the community. The challenge is how to make whole community worship accessible without excluding or being condescending.

At the heart of this challenge is the collective will to live lovingly, not as a fancy ideal on our lips, but worked out in the messy practical business of getting on with one another, respecting one another's validity, listening to one another, helping one another out, enabling without trying to take over, giving both space and support to one another. I'm talking church congregation, here. It's about learning to love those other people in our church community – not expecting someone else to take the annoying ones out of our hair, or expecting the rest of the community to toe the line with what we ourselves want.

We will never learn this kind of loving unless we get into the habit of practising, and that is why you will find I have provided plenty of opportunity for mixed age groups to work together, rather than suggesting completely different programmes for each age. Let's work together at breaking down some of these artificial barriers between age groups which we are taught to build. The very process of working together like this is all part of the Advent journey – as we learn to become a community of love, learning to watch and wait and wonder together.

Throughout this book there are mixed-age-group activities and times of worship and reflection which happen in the formal setting of a church congregation, and others which keep the Advent pulse going on a daily basis, in homes and households, in family or friendship groups, or alone.

Yes, it's difficult. Yes, it goes against the grain. But it's fully and gloriously in line with the outrageous kind of loving, forgiving community we are called to be if we are ever to be salt and light.

December – the Advent season – is one of those rare times when it's OK to talk about Jesus as an integral part of life, so a church community Advent experience is properly counter-cultural, living out our calling to be a sign of the kingdom right in the heart of the culture we inhabit.

Sharing an Advent meal

This can be a family or household meal at home, or a few invited friends, a class project or a whole parish event. You might decide to make this a weekly event, trying one eating idea during each of the four Advent weeks, or have one special meal during the season.

Keep all planning and preparation to a minimum to avoid adding to people's workload. 'Bring and share' works efficiently for a larger scale event.

Here are a few suggestions to start you thinking . . .

Food

Taster clues

Make a starter from small amounts of main course ingredients arranged separately on a saucer, so people can try to guess what's coming. (If the main meal is pasta with sauce and a salad, the saucer might have on it a slice of tomato, a piece of pasta, a little grated cheese, salt, and a sprig of parsley or basil.) In the middle of each saucer place a Bible reference of a prophecy. As people guess from the food clues what the meal will be, they look up the prophecies and think how they were fulfilled in Jesus, and/or have yet to be fulfilled.

- Isaiah 11:1-2
- Isaiah 35:5
- Psalm 146:7
- Isaiah 7:14
- Isaiah 65:17
- Daniel 12:1-2
- Micah 5:2
- Micah 5:4-5
- Malachi 4:5-6

Arrow biscuits

Either make arrow-shaped biscuits with a hole in, or buy biscuits with holes, such as party rings or brandy snaps. Roll up pieces of paper and fix them in the holes. On the paper is written a verse from scripture describing what God is like.

- Psalm 3:5
- Psalm 9:9
- Psalm 10:17-18
- Psalm 23:1
- Psalm 32:4-5
- Psalm 34:18
- Psalm 36:5-6
- Psalm 100:5
- Psalm 103:8
- Psalm 104:24
- Psalm 116:5
- Psalm 116:8
- Psalm 139:3-4
- Psalm 147:3

Hidden secrets

Choose food which has something hidden which you only find in the eating. This might be sweets with special centres, jam or apple doughnuts, toad in the hole, scotch eggs or mince pies. You could also make up dishes with hidden surprises inside – such as jelly into which you press jelly babies just before the jelly is completely set, or an olive or whole tomato stirred into a cauliflower cheese. On or by the serving dishes place these words:

- 'Now I know in part; then I shall know fully, just as I am fully known.' *1 Corinthians 13:12*
- 'There is nothing hidden that will not be made known.' *Luke 12:2*
- 'Then the glory of the Lord shall be revealed, and all people shall see it together.' *Isaiah 40:5*
- 'But about that day or hour no one knows, neither the angels in heaven, nor the Son, but only the Father. Beware, keep alert; for you do not know when the time will come.' *Mark 13:32-33*

Last things

Advent is a time to think about those important and often 'unfashionable' or even taboo areas of Death, Judgement, Heaven and Hell. But for the faith community of the church it doesn't have to be like that. With our hope of life that does not finish at death, we can feel safe enough through God's love and grace to face these important issues naturally and even with a healthy sense of humour.

Mould marzipan or white icing into skull shapes, serve frothy heavenly clouds of meringue, or lemon mousse, fresh herbs as the leaves for the healing of the nations, and fruit from the tree of life. Red peppers, tomatoes, beetroot, carrot sticks and radishes can be arranged like the fires of hell. For 'judgement' have a pair of scales on the table and a bowl of maltesers or raisins available. Each person takes a ball of red coloured marzipan and shapes it into a heart. They use this as a weight on the scales and measure out the matching weight of maltesers or raisins. Here are the quotations to go with the dishes:

- 'You have been weighed on the scales and found not good enough.' *Daniel 5:27*
- 'Not everyone who says to me, "Lord, Lord," will enter the kingdom of heaven, but only he who does the will of my Father who is in heaven.' *Matthew 7:21*
- 'I tell you, my friends, do not be afraid of those who kill the body and after that can do no more. But I will show you whom you should fear: fear him who, after the killing of the body, has power to throw you into hell. Yes, I tell you, fear him. Are not five sparrows sold for two pennies? Yet not one of them is forgotten by God. Indeed, the very hairs of your head are all numbered. Don't be afraid; you are worth more than many sparrows.' *Luke 12:4-7*

Table decorations

- Traditionally the Advent colour is purple, so use this colour for cloths and napkins.
- Provide crowns to be decorated and then worn while eating.
- Paint the borders of white paper plates.
- Cut doilies from purple and silver paper.

- Give people purple and silver paper crowns to wear.
- Have lots of candlelight among the dishes and stuck into cakes and pies.

Saying grace

A grace to sing, to the tune of 'Twinkle, twinkle, little star':

Thank you for this food to eat,
fresh and tasty, savoury, sweet.
In this Advent time we pray:
feed us with your love each day;
may the love you freely give
make us loving as we live. Amen.

A grace to say:

Heavenly Father,
during this Advent season
we thank you for feeding us
in body, mind and spirit. Amen.

Opening Advent windows

Most homes and some classrooms and offices have an Advent calendar with windows to open each day. Whatever kind of Advent calendar you have, you can use these daily readings as a family or class activity.

Leader   God loves us and knows us all by name . . .

All say your names – one by one if there are only a few of you, all together if there are lots.

Leader   Together we have come to worship you.

Everyone   Glory to God in the highest!

Whoever's turn it is to open the day's window, opens it now, and the day's reading is read aloud.

Everyone   Thanks be to God. Amen.

The daily readings

Day 1 – Genesis 1:1
In the beginning God created the heavens and the earth.

Day 2 – Genesis 1:31
God saw everything that he had made and indeed it was very good.

Day 3 – Psalm 18:28
It is you who lights my lamp; the Lord my God lights up my darkness.

Day 4 – Psalm 51:10
Create in me a clean heart, O God, and put a new and right spirit within me.

Day 5 – Psalm 55:16

I call upon God and the Lord will save me.

Day 6 – Isaiah 25:9

This is the Lord for whom we have waited. Let us be glad and rejoice that he saves us.

Day 7 – Isaiah 33:22

The Lord is our King; he will save us.

Day 8 – Isaiah 35:4

Say to those who are of a fearful heart, 'Be strong, do not fear! Here is your God.'

Day 9 – Isaiah 43:1

Do not fear, for I have redeemed you. I have called you by name, you are mine.

Day 10 – Isaiah 60:1

Arise, shine; for your light has come and the glory of the Lord has risen upon you.

Day 11 – John 1:9

The true light, which lights up everyone, was coming into the world.

Day 12 – Luke 1:30

Do not be afraid, Mary, for you have found favour with God.

Day 13 – Luke 1:31

You will bear a son and you will call him Jesus.

Day 14 – Luke 1:32

He will be great and will be called the Son of the Most High.

Day 15 – Luke 1:46-47

And Mary said . . . 'My spirit rejoices in God my Saviour.'

Day 16 – Matthew 1:20

Joseph, son of David, do not be afraid to take Mary as your wife.

Day 17 – Matthew 1:21

She will bear a son and you are to name him Jesus for he will save his people from their sins.

Day 18 – Luke 2:4

Joseph went to be registered at Bethlehem with Mary who was expecting a baby.

Day 19 – Luke 2:7

While they were there she gave birth to her firstborn son.

Day 20 – Luke 2:7

She wrapped the baby in bands of cloth and laid him in a manger because there was no room in the inn.

Day 21 – Luke 2:8

There were shepherds living in the fields, keeping watch over their flocks by night.

Day 22 – Luke 2:9

An angel of the Lord appeared, and the glory of the Lord shone around them, and they were terrified.

Day 23 – Luke 2:11

The angel said, 'To you is born this day in the city of David a Saviour, who is the Messiah, the Lord.'

Day 24 – Luke 2:16

So they hurried off and found Mary and Joseph and the child lying in the manger.

Day 25 – John 1:14

The Word became flesh and lived among us, and we have seen his glory.

Making an Advent wreath

Many churches have an Advent wreath, but you can easily make one for your home or school. It could be placed in the centre of the table for a mealtime or in the hall for assembly.

The idea of the wreath is that as we look forward to the coming of Jesus, the Light of the World, we light another candle each week of waiting, so that the light gets brighter the closer we get to Christmas. On Christmas Day all the candles are lit, including the one in the middle.

> **Take great care with candles and never leave them burning unattended!**

How to make an Advent wreath

You will need . . .

- A foil dish
- A block of oasis for fresh flowers
- Five candles, with one of them white or decorated
- Greenery and flowers

What you do . . .

1. Soak the oasis in water.
2. Press it into the foil dish so that it's wedged in.
3. Press in four candles around the outside and the white or decorated one in the middle.
4. Poke leaves and flowers into the oasis around the candles so that it's covered up and looks nice from all sides.
5. The first Sunday (or week) in Advent you light one candle, the second Sunday two candles, the third Sunday three candles and the fourth Sunday four candles. On Christmas Day light all five candles.

Songs for lighting the Advent candles

Try lighting the candles when it's really dark and see what a difference the light makes, even with just one candle burning! Here are some ideas for songs to sing as you do it . . .

To the tune 'She'll be coming round the mountain':

O the light of God was coming to the world,
O the light of God was coming to the world.
It was coming as a baby,
a little tiny baby.
The light of God was coming to the world!

To the tune 'She'll be coming round the mountain':

May the light of God shine brighter in our lives,
may the light of God shine brighter in our lives.
Light us up and make us loving,
a people who are loving.
May the light of God shine brighter in our lives!

To the tune of 'Frère Jacques':

Light a candle, light a candle,
let it shine! Let it shine!
Like the love of Jesus, like the love of Jesus,
let it shine! Let it shine!

To the tune of 'Frère Jacques':

Advent candles, Advent candles,
burning bright, burning bright,
lighting up our darkness, lighting up our darkness
with God's light, with God's light.

Advent wreaths in church

Usually the five candles are already in place, with an extra one lit each week. Another way of using the wreath is to start on Advent Sunday with none of the candles on it. The first lit candle is processed through the church during the first reading – perhaps by a young person dressed in a white garment.

For each week of Advent another candle is carried through the church in procession to join those already lit, so that the link between prophecy and growing enlightenment is visually made.

An alternative way of doing this is to have one candle brought in procession the first week, two the second, and so on, so that the accumulating brightness is there in the procession as well as on the wreath.

Making an Advent candle calendar

You can buy Advent candles in the shops, which are marked with numbers up to 25. You burn the candle down just a little each day through Advent, like a kind of shining calendar. These candles are not too hard to make, but you will need to be very careful.

> **Adult supervision needed.**

You will need . . .
- A tall candle
- A ruler
- A knife
- Poster paints and brush

What you do . . .
1. Protect the working area with newspaper or plastic bin-bags.
2. Lay the candle down along the edge of the ruler.
3. Starting at the end of the candle with the wick, use the knife to mark off 25 1cm lengths. (You don't have to write on any numbers.)
4. Hold the knife against the candle as you roll it round, so that the scored marks go all the way round the candle each time.
5. Paint each section in bright colours so it's easy to see where the sections start and end.
6. If you want numbers, draw them on with a black pen.

Lighting the Advent candle calendar

The best time to light your Advent candle calendar each day is when it's dark. Light it when you start to say your bedtime prayers, or when you start a bedtime story, and blow it out when it burns down to where the colour changes. The shorter your candle gets, the nearer it must be to Christmas!

You could sing one of the Advent wreath songs, or one of these . . .

To the tune of 'See saw, Marjorie Daw':

> Jesus, Jesus,
> Coming to earth as a baby,
> Jesus, Jesus,
> Coming to earth as a baby.

To the tune from Beethoven's Pastoral Symphony, 'Thanksgiving after the storm':

> God comes to save us,
> he comes to set us free,
> he loves us, he loves us,
> for all eternity.

To the tune of 'EastEnders':

> Candle burning in the night,
> showing us the light
> of Jesus our Saviour.
> Candle burning in the night,
> tell us of the Light
> which shines in our world with love.

Morning prayers for Advent

The world moves round into the light of the day
and we thank you, Father, that we are alive in it.
In this Advent season of watching and waiting,
keep us attentive to you, throughout the day,
ready to listen, ready to learn and ready to love.
Amen.

Anchor me, Lord God,
and keep me firmly fixed
in the depth of your love.
Amen.

In this dark time of the year
we are reminded of our need for light.
Prepare our hearts to hold more love,
so that the world's darkness may grow less
and the light of love shine brighter.
Amen.

Where we are cold and in darkness
warm and brighten us.
Where we are forgetful of our calling
remind and refresh us.
Where we have lost hope
revive and restore us.
Where we have lost our way
find us and set us once again
on the path of life.
Amen.

Night prayers for Advent

As I lie down to rest and sleep
guard and protect me through the night.
Watch over me and those I love,
and bring us safe to the morning light.
Amen.

Through the generations
your people waited in hope and expectation.
Now in the darkness of this Advent night
we re-live that waiting with them,
re-live that small bright hope
as it brightens into the full glory
'as of the only begotten of the Father –
full of grace and truth'.
Amen. Come, Lord Jesus!

Darkness of night . . . darkness of death . . .
Lord in heaven, give us grace
to face the truth of our mortality
and worship you, the Immortal.
May your life, lodged richly in ours,
show us death in the context of eternity,
that we may know your peace, now and always.
Amen.

May the darkness of the worldly
never shut out
the light of the Godly,
lit at creation and ever brightening.
Amen.

'Open church' days in Advent

There are many people who feel ill at ease with the concept of 'churchgoing' for all kinds of reasons, but who like to wander around an open church looking and listening, or just taking time to be still in a holy place.

Rather than always thinking we must encourage people to come to an actual church service, we can respond to the spiritual hunger of an 'unchurched' generation simply by opening our churches up more often. Allow the church building and the holy space to do the speaking. Prepare a landscape which is conducive to worship and prayer, and allow people to come in and out in their 'browsing' way, content for God to draw them into a sense of his presence.

Advent is a particularly good time to try such 'open church' days, as people are generally both stressed and needing places of peace, and also prepared to think about Jesus more than at other times of year.

Here are some ideas to get you started. Do please take them as starters and adapt and change them to suit your particular area and building.

Planning and mapping

- Gather two or three of you, representative of different age groups, and wander around the church, praying. You might like to do this in silence, or put some music on quietly. Then gather around a flipchart page of paper with some Post-its in two different colours and felt-tip pens and draw a rough outline of the church. As a title write: **How does our building help us to worship in Advent?**
- Write or draw all the ideas on one colour Post-its, sticking them on to the appropriate places. Share the ideas and celebrate them.
- Now edit the title to read: **How could our building help visitors to worship in Advent?** On the other colour Post-its scribble all the ideas. You'll find that once someone has one creative, good idea loads of other possibilities start popping up. The different age groups encourage a far broader range of ideas.

- Use this map to plan four open church times during the Advent season. You don't have to use all the ideas every time, of course – you may decide to take one suggestion and keep it going for each of the sessions, shifting the emphasis in some way as the season progresses; or you might have some different ideas for each week.

General guidelines

- Always remember that we are doing this to help people encounter God, so don't let any activity or decoration get in the way of this.
- Choose accompanying music which isn't intrusive but helps establish a sense of quietness and wonder, worship and mystery. It doesn't have to be specifically Christian music, though, of course, this works very well. Music from film soundtracks can be effective, as can natural sounds, such as birdsong, or the sound of the sea.
- Bear in mind the kind of people who may be coming in, and their particular needs. If you are near a shopping centre, for instance, there may need to be a safe place for bags to be checked in, so people can move around more freely. If children are likely to wander in unaccompanied, have teenagers or adults to accompany them around the church.
- Make sure that signs are large enough to be read easily whatever your height, and whether or not you are a wheelchair user. Accompany words with symbols or pictures where possible to help non-readers.
- It's useful to have 'prayer trail' guides available for people to take around the church with them, rather like you might be given at an art exhibition or in a nature reserve.
- Have large notices explaining that this is a holy place where for (hundreds of) years people have met with God in prayer and worship. Invite them to share the peace of the place and touch base with their soul.
- Don't expect to get everything right first time. Don't let your personal investment in the project blind you to what needs tweaking or changing completely. Build ongoing assessment and development into the overall programme, and allow God to teach you through the process.

'Open church' ideas with an Advent flavour

- Use the Advent colour of purple all around the church, perhaps with increasing silver or white as you get closer to Christmas. Use it not only for the altar frontal and lectern, but in any background paper or fabric for other focuses of worship or reflection.

- **The font.** Focus here on John the Baptist preparing the people for the coming of the Messiah, giving them 'a working knowledge of salvation by the forgiveness of all their sins'. You might have pictures of John baptising in the river Jordan, accounts of this for different age groups and Bibles available with references to look up. Fill the font with water and have a fresh white towel beside it. On a card nearby suggest that people may like to put things right with God, recognising what needs forgiving and washing their hands in the font as a sign that they are sorry and are asking for God's forgiveness. Have the words of forgiveness written on small cards for them to take away as a reminder of God's forgiving love.

- **Stained glass windows.** Either through a display nearby, or by the 'prayer trail' guide, draw people's attention to particular details of the window and give a simple version of the story it tells, or the life of the saint it portrays. Add a prayer they can use and an activity or response, such as colouring a print-out of the window, standing in the light from the window and imagining standing in the light of God's love, or looking up an appropriate Bible reference (such as Matthew 5:16; Ephesians 5:8; Psalm 104:2; Luke 2:9).

- **Lectern.** On printed card, or in the prayer trail guide, people are invited to read the passage of the Bible left open (give exact chapter and verses). Nearby are bubble writing print-outs (or one large one on lining paper) of a particular verse with sponges and paint trays, or crayons or scrunched tissue paper for everyone to add to, so that it is being communally decorated as people let the words soak into them. Choose the actual passage from among the week's readings.

- **Prayer stations.** In several places around the church set up areas of focus for prayer, using perhaps draped fabric, some candles on a mirror, a globe, images and headlines from newspapers and charity magazines, and printed suggestions for prayer. Create a display which helps people focus their prayer, gives them guidance but still leaves them free to do the praying themselves, in their own way. If you have an east-end altar which is not often used now, make one of these prayer stations up in this part of the church. Others might be in a side chapel or near the side walls of the church. Keep the Advent themes going, with one prayer repeated in all of them, but otherwise make them all different – rather as flower arrangements might be presented during a flower festival. Include pens with Post-its or candle-shapes of paper for people to write their own prayers if they wish.

- **Doors.** Have a copy of Holman Hunt's picture 'The Light of the World' fixed to the door or displayed close by. Direct people's attention to the clues which show the door hasn't been opened for some time, and ask where the door's handle is. By getting people to look at the meaning behind the picture, you are helping them come naturally to consider the Advent message of Jesus, the Light of the World, standing at the door of our hearts and knocking. Have a 'thought-bubble' board nearby for people to write their thoughts about the picture. Of course, there are plenty of other works of art to use in the same way.

- **Prayer book.** Have a large and beautifully bound book, with a variety of coloured paper, pens and stickers available at a table. Invite people to write or draw their prayers and stick them in the book. It's a good idea to have already completed a few, so that people can see some ideas. Don't make all these examples so perfect that people are discouraged from having a go. And although most visitors may well think of this as a children's activity, it isn't at all reserved for children, so indicate this by the examples provided.

- Protect the floor area and have plenty of plant pots, earth and a basket of bulbs. Provide freezer labels and coloured pens as well. Display in large print a Bible verse homing in on the idea of secret growing which eventually becomes gloriously visible. For instance, both in written form and verbally, invite people to pray as they plant a bulb, decorate a label and take the pot home with them. Caring for the bulb and enjoying its flower will be a prayer reminder.

- **Recorded prayers, readings and music.** Lend personal tape/CD players for people to listen to. You can either make use of commercially produced resources, such as *Footprints* or *Telling* *the story* or spoken Bible tapes, or you could create your own, perhaps with different age groups working on something with their own particular cultural flavour.

- **Your own church's particular features.** What I have suggested in all of these is inevitably generalised. But you will be able to adapt them and also to use other features of your particular building to help those of all ages to engage in conversation with God, even if they are not normally used to praying. Don't forget to look up as well as around when you are planning what to include.

An Advent Sunday candlelit vigil: 'Hope in the darkness'

Advent Sunday evening is an opportunity to set the mood of the season with a service of darkness and candlelight, penitence and forgiveness, hope and promise. After the sad and solemn mood of November, with the nights drawing in and cold weather taking hold, Advent is fresh and expectant, with a sense of excitement in the waiting and preparation.

It may seem strange to have a service of this penitential and solemn nature as an all-age occasion, but it is important that our young people are included in the community for these times of searching questions – indeed, it is often the young children who come out with all those questions about death and heaven, while the adults spend much energy avoiding them at all costs. Part of taking our children seriously as members of the faith community is not shutting them off from large chunks of the gospel. Rather, our responsibility is to stand alongside them as we all learn more about God's love and forgiveness, about the matters of earth and heaven, life and death, good and evil.

This script includes short interviews, sketches and activities which link the readings with their Advent theme. Each person present will need a card circle candle protector, and a candle. Alternatively, it would be quite appropriate to use the Christingle at the service. In this case adapt the 'time to think a bit' section.

The card circles are given out as people come into church. Prepare them beforehand with a perforated cross shape in the centre. (Stand each circle on a pad of blutack or plastic modelling clay, and make holes along the lines of a cross using a sharp pencil.)

Have the candles ready in a number of small baskets, in order to give them out during the service as easily and quickly as possible.

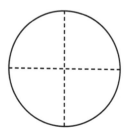

Hope in the darkness

Five tall, unlit candles are arranged, like the five dots on dice, in the front centre of the building. The church is in darkness, as far as possible, and as people gather there is recorded music playing, music which speaks of ache and longing. The soundtracks from Schindler's List, Gladiator *or* Lord of the Rings *work well. So does the hauntingly beautiful music of plainsong, by composers such as Thomas Tallis, with all the many layers of voice parts. There is even a gorgeous combination of plainsong and Jan Garbarek saxophone called 'Remember me, my dear' by the Hilliard Ensemble, which would cry into the darkness of a lofty building with great power.*

The music dies away into silence.

Script 1

The child and the man are not visible.

Child's voice   Daddy, where are you? . . . I can't see you . . . The darkness is hiding you.

Man's voice   Don't be afraid – I am here with you. The darkness is hiding me, but I'm still here. Don't be afraid. Don't be afraid.

The five candles in the centre of the front of the church are lit.

Reading 1

During the reading four people of different age groups each take a candle and walk with it north, south, east and west, to the walls of the church, and stand the candles there. Then enough lights are switched on for people to read words.

The child and the man stand and read together

In the beginning
God created the heavens and the earth.

Now the earth was formless and empty,
darkness was over the surface of the deep,
and the Spirit of God was hovering over the waters.
And God said,
'LET THERE BE LIGHT!'
and there was light.
God saw that the light was good,
and he separated the light from the darkness.
God called the light 'day', and the darkness he
    called 'night'.
And there was evening, and there was morning –
    the first day.
(*Genesis 1:1-5, NIV*)

A hymn is sung. Suggestions:

- Be still, for the presence of the Lord
- Lord of the future, Lord of the past
- As we are gathered, Jesus is here
- Father, we love you

Script 2

Two young people in conversation. They are walking up the centre of the church as they talk.

First   I can see it's a beautiful world. But if God made it, and God's good, why is there so much pain and evil?

Second   Yes, that's what I find hard to cope with. Why doesn't God stop the bad things happening? Why does he let us keep messing things up for one another?

First   I suppose he's treating us with respect in a way – you know, giving us the freedom to make our own choices and all that.

Second   The trouble is, if I'm honest I know I often choose what *I* want, even if it might be a pain for someone else.

First   God seems to want us to be loving, like he is, but he makes it really difficult for us, doesn't he?

Second   Well, I guess loving *is* really difficult, isn't it?

Reading 2

An adult reads this, as much as possible as if they are speaking it, rather than reading it. If it is very thoroughly prepared beforehand, they will be able to bring the words to life (it was, after all, Joshua's speech to the people) and use hands and body in the telling.

This command I give you today is not too hard for you. It is not beyond what you can do. It is not up in heaven. You do not have to ask, 'Who will go up to heaven and get it for us so we can obey it and keep it?' It is not on the other side of the sea. You do not have to ask, 'Who will go across the sea and get it? Who will tell it to us so we can keep it?' No, the Word is very near you. It is in your mouth and in your heart so you may obey it. Today I ask heaven and earth to be witnesses. I am offering you life or death, blessings or curses. Now choose life! Then you and your children may live. Love the Lord your God. Obey him. Stay close to him. He is your life.
(*Deuteronomy 30:11-14, 19-20a, based on* International Children's Bible)

The summary of the Law is taught and sung first all together and then in a round, to the tune of 'London's Burning'. Include a round of actions as well if you wish.

You shall love the Lord your God with
(*hand on heart then point up*)

31

all your heart and all your mind and
> *(one hand on heart, other pats it in a pulse,*
> *then both hands hold head)*

all your strength! All your strength!
> *(Flex biceps)*

And love your neighbour, and love your neighbour.
> *(Hold hands with neighbour on each side in turn)*

Time to think a bit . . .

Ask everyone to hold the card circle they were given as they came in. Like the beautiful planet we have been given to live in, it's round.

We all live on the outside edge of our planet earth. Tracing our fingers around the outside of the circle, we'll take a quick journey all round the world . . . Starting wherever you are, take them on a whistle-stop tour of mountains, rainforests, deserts, seas and oceans and islands, and back to their seat in church. It certainly is a beautiful world God has made!

Now look at the perforated cross shape in the middle. If we are going to be able to love, we must be free to make our own choices. Otherwise we'd just be puppets. And often we make bad choices, and choose what is wrong and unkind. We spoil what God has made good.

Invite everyone to push their finger through the perforated cross and make a hole in the circle. Living like this makes us unhappy, makes others suffer, and makes God sad. God sees when we are kind and loving. God sees when we are not. And when we die, we will see God face to face. We won't be able to pretend about who we are and how we have lived. God knows us completely, the bad as well as the good in us.

So we need to tell God we are sorry for our selfishness and sin. We need to reject evil and turn to God, asking him to forgive us and heal our world. As we listen to the next reading, we'll hold this broken circle in our hands and remember that God knows us completely.

Reading 3

Have some reflective music playing quietly from before the reading starts to after it ends. If you are able to, project an image of a newborn baby, or hands shaping clay.

Your hands shaped me and made me. Will you now turn and destroy me? Remember that you moulded me like a piece of clay. Will you now turn me back into dust? You formed me in my mother's womb as cheese is formed from milk. You put skin and flesh on me like clothing. You sewed me together with bones and muscles. You gave me life and showed me kindness and in your care you watched over my life. But in your heart you hid other plans. I know this was what was in your mind: If I sinned, you would be watching me. You would not let my sin go unpunished.

(*Job 10:8-15, based on* International Children's Bible)

Music fades into silence.

The words of God's forgiveness are spoken.

The God of love, who brought you to life and knows you completely, hears your longing for forgiveness, and reaches out his arms to welcome you and rescue you. Nothing and no one is beyond the power of his forgiveness. You are freed from all that is past, and he will walk with you in person through the rest of your life.
Amen.

Candles are given out. Invite everyone to push the candle through the hole in the circle of card. The candles are lit, as a sign of the way God's love shines out in us and in our world, healing what is broken, bringing the light of hope into the darkness of evil and suffering. If possible, have the lights off or dimmed and the words of the following worship projected, so everyone can hold their candle and sing at the same time.

A hymn is sung. Suggestions:
- I'm accepted, I'm forgiven
- I am a new creation
- O, heaven is in my heart
- I heard the voice of Jesus say

Script 3

A child and an elderly adult in conversation. Try sitting them on bar stools.

Child   I wonder what it will be like when we die.

Adult   Oh, you've got a long time before you need to think about things like that!

Child   But is it true that we all have to die?

Adult   Yes, it's true. We are all born into this world as babies, and one day we all die.

Child   Will Jesus welcome us into heaven when we die?

Adult   Do you want to go to heaven when you die, and be with Jesus for ever?

Child   Yes, I do. It sounds a happy place to be, and safe. And I love Jesus. He's kind and I can trust him.

Adult   In that case Jesus will be opening the doors of heaven wide for you! He isn't one to turn away any who want to be with him.

Reading 4

Everyone reads this together. Adults move their finger along the words to help young readers join in. Non-readers look at the picture below, and hear the words spoken. Or an image of shepherd and sheep and lambs could be projected.

> You are forgiving and good, O Lord, abounding in love to all who call to you. Hear my prayer, O Lord; listen to my cry for mercy. In the day of my trouble I will call to you, for you will answer me.
>
> Teach me your way, O Lord, and I will walk in your truth; give me an undivided heart, that I may fear your name. I will praise you, O Lord my God,

with all my heart; I will glorify your name for ever. For great is your love towards me; you have delivered me from the depths of the grave. You, O Lord, are a compassionate and gracious God, slow to anger, abounding in love and faithfulness.

(*From Psalm 86, NIV*)

Everyone holds their lighted Advent candles up as they sing this in a round, to the tune of 'Frère Jacques':

> Advent candles, Advent candles,
> burning bright, burning bright,
> lighting up our darkness, lighting up our darkness
> with God's light, with God's light.

Finish with a prayer:

> Another Advent has begun.
> Lord our God,
> lead us in the way of truth and love,

kindness and mercy.
As we get ready for Christmas,
may we learn more about loving you
and loving one another.
Give us courage to keep asking
the big questions about life and death,
knowing that you are in our past, our present and
    all our future.
You know us completely and you love us
    completely.
Thank you, Lord God, for making us,
and for coming to be born among us as a baby.
May we worship you with our whole lives.
Amen.

The candles are blown out. Full lights come on.

A final hymn is sung. Suggestions:

- O come, O come, Emmanuel
- Praise my soul the King of heaven
- Immortal, invisible
- O Lord my God (How great thou art)

An Advent carol service
in the week before Christmas

By this stage in Advent the brightness of the Christmas season is approaching. There is often a concern to use this outreach possibility, but at the same time everyone is busy and there isn't a lot of time for rehearsals.

This late Advent service is designed to give a fresh and rather unusual slant to the story of God's salvation, focusing on the gradually unfolding plan of Incarnation, rather than on the nativity. It is not a children's nativity play, and the characters are best played by age-appropriate adults – for example, a teenage young woman as Mary and an elderly couple as Zechariah and Elizabeth.

The service might begin with mulled wine / fruit juice and mince pies as the shopping draws to a close on the Saturday before Christmas . . .

At the front of the church create the impression of a beautiful garden, with a 'fence' around it. You could use the sanctuary as the garden area and the communion rail as the fence. You need to make a flaming sword which is fixed, blade pointing upwards, to the gate in the fence. During the final scripted interview Mary, holding the child Jesus, will need to take this sword off and turn it upside down, so that it looks like a cross.

Characters can be dressed up, but don't need to learn lines. Give everyone clipboards with their scripts on. This is written into the text.

Order of service

1. Carol: 'O come, O come, Emmanuel'
2. Welcome and prayer
3. First reading: Genesis 3:20-24 (*The Armed Man*: Track 3)
4. Interview 1
5. Carol or hymn
6. Interview 2
7. Second reading: Luke 1:26-38 (*Lord of the Rings*: Track 1)
8. Carol or hymn
9. Interview 3
10. Third reading: Luke 1:67-68, 76-79 (*Schindler's List*: Track 4)
11. Carol or hymn
12. Interview 4
13. Fourth reading: Luke 2:1, 3-7 (*The Armed Man*: Track 1)
14. Carol or hymn
15. Interview 5
16. Fifth reading: Luke 2:8-20 (*Lord of the Rings*: Track 1)
17. Carol or hymn
18. Interview 6
19. Carol or hymn
20. Prayer and blessing
21. Carol: 'O come, all ye faithful'

First reading – Genesis 3:20-24

This is read by a group of speakers, all together. They think like a choir, and need to practise together well, so rests are taken and emphasis placed appropriately. It builds to a strong finish.

(The Armed Man: Track 3)

The man named his wife *(Pause)* Eve *(Pause)* because she would become the mother of all the living. The Lord God made garments of animal skins for Adam and his wife and clothed them. *(Pause)* And the Lord God said, 'The man has now become like one of us, knowing good <u>and</u> evil. He must not be allowed to reach out his hand and take also from the tree of life and eat, and live for ever.' *(Pause while music continues)*

So the Lord God <u>banished</u> him from the Garden of Eden to work the ground from which he had been taken. *(Pause)* After he drove the man out, he placed on the east side of the Garden of Eden *(Get louder from here to the end)* cherubim and a flaming sword flashing back and forth to guard the way to the <u>tree</u> <u>of</u> life.

Interview 1

(Eve is sitting outside the garden)

Mary   Ah, there you are, Eve! I've been looking for you everywhere. We're doing this documentary for the BBC and I wanted to interview a woman who's been locked out. You seemed the obvious choice. How does it feel, being locked out of the Garden of Eden?

Eve   *(Looks at her suspiciously)* Are you human?

Mary   Yes, of course I'm human – I'm as human as you are.

Eve   In that case I imagine you know exactly what it feels like, 'cause we humans are all in the same mess, aren't we? – locked out from where we belong and wishing we weren't. Do you know what I've discovered?

Mary   What?

Eve   If you're locked out from where you really want to be, then you're in a kind of prison. You know why we're locked out of the garden, do you?

Mary   Something to do with a snake and an apple, wasn't it?

Eve   Yeah, they came into it, but it's all about those two trees.

Mary   Which two trees?

Eve   Right in the middle of that garden there's two trees, right? There's the tree of the knowledge of good and evil . . .

Mary   . . . that's the one you were told not to eat and ended up eating?

Eve   That's the one . . . and another tree – the tree of life. Now that humans know about good *and* evil, God

40

	can't risk us eating from the tree of life, can he, or there'd be no hope for us at all, would there? I mean, we'd be in this mess for ever with no way out.
Mary	But you must miss the garden?
Eve	Yes, of course I do! You know what it's like – all you really want is to be back in the garden, living for ever in peace and happiness, like it was in the beginning.
Mary	What about God – does he ignore you now you're locked out here?
Eve	Oh no, he loves us, you see. He watches over us all the time and cheers us up when we get discouraged. He'd love us to be able to enjoy the garden with him . . . You know what?
Mary	What?
Eve	I have a hope that one day a human will be born who can open the garden to us again. I can't imagine how. But I just wish it could happen.
Mary	You're getting discouraged again, Eve. See if this song helps . . .

A song or carol is sung. Suggestions:
- He's got the whole world in his hands
- The universe was waiting
- The King of Love my shepherd is

Interview 2

Eve   Look, can I have a go with that thing and interview you now, Mary?

Mary   Well . . . I don't know that the BBC will . . .

Eve   Oh, go on – it'll make their ratings rocket!

Mary   OK. Here you are.

Eve   So, Mary, are you married?

Mary   No, not yet.

Eve   And you're expecting, right?

Mary   Right.

Eve   Boyfriend still with you, is he?

Mary   Well, he wasn't planning to be once he found out about the baby. But then he changed his mind.

Eve   Mm. God have a quiet word in his ear, did he?

Mary   Yes, as a matter of fact he did. My Joe had a dream of an angel who put his mind at rest. Explained that I hadn't been unfaithful to him, the child was a child of God's promise. So he's being really supportive now.

Eve   So was that true about the baby's father?

Mary   I know it sounds odd, but it's what happened. An angel came to see me a few months ago, you see, and . . . well, listen.

Second reading – Luke 1:26-38

In the sixth month, God sent the angel Gabriel to a virgin pledged to be married to a man named Joseph, a descendant of David. The virgin's name was Mary.

(Lord of the Rings: Track 1)

The angel went to her and said, 'Greetings, you who are highly favoured! The Lord is with you.'

Mary was greatly troubled at his words and wondered what kind of greeting this might be.

But the angel said to her, 'Do not be afraid, Mary, you have found favour with God. You will be with child and give birth to a son, and you are to give him the name Jesus. He will be great and will be called the Son of the Most High. The Lord God will give him the throne of his father David, and he will reign over the house of Jacob for ever; his kingdom will never end.'

'How will this be,' Mary asked the angel, 'since I am a virgin?'

The angel answered, 'The Holy Spirit will come upon you, and the power of the Most High will overshadow you. So the holy one to be born will be called the Son of God. Even Elizabeth your relative is going to have a child in her old age, and she who was said to be barren is in her sixth month of pregnancy. For nothing is impossible with God.'

(Music quietens)

'I am the Lord's servant,' Mary answered. 'May it be to me as you have said.'

Then the angel left her.

(Fade music)

Interview 3

Eve You must be mad, agreeing to that, Mary! But then, on the other hand, perhaps you're not mad. Perhaps you're just the person God needs for the job of raising his Son. Who's that relative of yours the angel mentioned – Elizabeth, was it?

(Zechariah and Elizabeth come in, with Elizabeth holding a baby)

Elizabeth Yes, dear, Elizabeth. Oh, I know what you're thinking – we're a bit old for this sort of thing, aren't we? But there you are – another miracle! This is John, by the way. Say hello to Eve, John. She's your great, great, great, great . . .

Eve Oh, stop it – or we'll never get to the end of this play!

Mary My cousin Zechariah – Elizabeth's husband – is a priest, you know, and he saw an angel as well, a few months before me.

(Zechariah is smiling and miming his responses, but doesn't say anything)

Eve Popping up everywhere, aren't they?

Elizabeth and Mary Well, it is nearly Christmas!

Eve So was it one of those hard-up British students selling their eggs for elderly couples?

Elizabeth and Mary (Sternly) EVE!

(Zechariah looks suitably shocked)

Eve Sorry, just joking. Seriously, though, did your old man believe his old lady was going to have a baby?

Elizabeth   No, my dear, he didn't. Knocked him speechless it did *(Zechariah nods)* till the baby was born and named. But you know God – with him anything's possible. Listen. This is what my Zech said when our baby John here was born and named.

Third reading – Luke 1:67-68, 76-79

Read by a narrator and Zechariah

(Schindler's List: Track 4 – fade in slowly)

Narrator   When the baby was born, and named 'John', his father, Zechariah, was filled with the Holy Spirit and prophesied:

Zechariah   Praise be to the Lord, the God of Israel, because he has come and has redeemed his people . . .

(Now Zechariah takes the baby and addresses him)

And you – my child – will be called the prophet of the Most High. For you will go before the Lord to prepare the way for him, to give his people a working knowledge of salvation by the forgiveness of all their sins.

In the tender compassion of our God, the dawn from heaven will break upon us, to shine on those who live in darkness and under the shadow of death, and to guide our feet into the way of peace.

(Zechariah, Elizabeth and John leave; music fades out)

Interview 4

Eve   Won't it be lovely for you two to be together when Mary's baby is born!

Mary   I wish! But Joseph and I will be miles away from Elizabeth – we'll be in Bethlehem.

Eve   Really? Special offer on EasyJet, is it? A few days away on your own before all the broken nights and nappies?

Mary   Listen, Eve. You know what it's like to be locked out of the garden, but we're locked into our own country, as well, because we're living under occupation. If the Romans tell us to move we have to move, baby or no baby. We've got a 70-mile journey on foot to do for a Roman census – it's a massive headcount they're doing. Nothing we can do about it. Listen.

Fourth reading – Luke 2:1, 3-7

If possible make a recording of a young baby's cry to play during this reading. I have also used the baby crying and the applause from the soundtrack of a Vicar of Dibley *video.*

(The Armed Man: Track 1)

> In those days Caesar Augustus issued a decree that a census should be taken of the entire Roman world. And everyone went to his own town to register.
>
> So Joseph also went up from the town of Nazareth in Galilee to Judea, to Bethlehem – the town of David – because he belonged to the house and line of King David. He went there to register with Mary, who was pledged to be married to him and was expecting a child.

(Music fades)

> While they were there, the time came for the baby to be born, and she gave birth to her firstborn (*Wait for baby's cry*) – a son!
>
> She wrapped him in swaddling clothes and laid him in a manger, because there was no room for them in the inn.

Interview 5

(Mary now has a baby instead of a bump)

Mary   So here he is, Eve – God, born as a human baby. Want a cuddle? *(Gives Jesus to Eve)* I'll hold your script for you.

Eve   *(holding the baby)* Oh, Mary, this is amazing! Amazing.

Mary   Guess who God told first, so they could be the first visitors?

Eve   I don't know – the mayor of Bethlehem? King Herod?

Mary   Come on, this is God we're talking about – 'looks not on the outward appearance but into the heart'. Guess again.

Eve   You don't mean he told the kind of people that the world locks out?

Mary   Got it in one! Shepherds! He told shepherds! Listen . . .

Fifth reading – Luke 2:8-20

And there were shepherds living out in the fields near by, keeping watch over their flocks at night.

(Lord of the Rings: Track 1 – fades in)

An angel of the Lord appeared to them, and the glory of the Lord shone around them, and they were terrified. But the angel said to them, 'Do not be afraid. I bring you good news of great joy that will be for all the people. Today in the town of King David a Saviour has been born to you; he is Christ the Lord. This will be a sign to you: You will find a baby wrapped in swaddling clothes and lying in a manger.'

Suddenly a great company of the heavenly host appeared with the angel, praising God and saying, 'Glory to God in the highest, and on earth peace to those on whom his favour rests.'

(Music fades out)

When the angels had left them and gone into heaven, the shepherds said to one another, 'Let's go to Bethlehem and see this thing that has happened, which the Lord has told us about.'

(Same music fades in again)

So they hurried off and found Mary and Joseph, and the baby, who was lying in the manger. When they had seen him they spread the word of what had been told them about this child, and all who heard it were amazed at what the shepherds said to them.

But Mary treasured all these things and pondered them in her heart. The shepherds returned, glorifying and praising God for all the things they had heard and seen, which were just as they had been told.

(Music fades out)

Interview 6

Eve   I knew it! I knew he'd do it! God's sorted it, hasn't he! A human being but God's Son. Jesus must be the one who'll be able to open up the garden, isn't he?

Mary   Yes, Eve. That's why he came. That's what Christmas is all about.

(As she speaks, she changes the sword to a cross, opens the gate and they walk into the garden)

Finish with a carol, a prayer and blessing and then a final carol. Suggestions:

- Hark, the herald angels sing
- How lovely on the mountains
- Let all mortal flesh keep silence
- O come, all ye faithful

All-age Sunday worship in Advent

The whole point of gathered worship is that God has invited us. We are both servants and guests. All of us are invited guests of God, and that includes the ones up front as well. We're not being invited by the vicar, or the churchwardens, or the church, but by God. And all of us present, whatever our status in society, our height or shoe size, are workers in this business of serving. It's an attitude of mind which affects what goes on. We are all there to engage with God, to be attentive to God, to learn the loving he made us for. And being together provides us with a perfect way to do this with our feet firmly on the ground.

It's important that the worship is accessible to everyone present, whatever their age. This means accepting that we will all respond in different ways according to our skills, personalities, age group and culture, and all genuine responses are valid, however different they may be from what we ourselves hold precious. So that makes it sacrificial, because it will involve us in those qualities of tolerance and forbearance and generosity of spirit which we all find difficult.

But that's what grace is all about. It is God's grace that will enable us to become the community of love we are called to be – a people full of grace.

For each of the Sundays in Advent I have suggested various ways to use the senses in our shared worship. Using what we share in common, as we respond in our different ways to God's invitation, enables us to be a whole community at worship together.

First Sunday of Advent, Years ABC

Focus of the service:
Watching and waiting. The patriarchs.

Mood:
Expectant. Honest. Time to wake up and get ready.

Possibilities for worship

- The words from the day's reading (such as Isaiah 2.5: 'Come, let us walk in the light of the Lord!') printed in bubble writing, with crayons and pens available.
- Paper, crayons, scissors and tape for drawing round feet, writing words from the readings and taping to the floor.
- Purple streamers and flags available to wave in worship during hymns.
- Instruments ready for accompanying the last hymn.
- CDs reflecting the mood and focus as people gather, during the time of penitence and intercession.
- Projected images of winter trees in a cold landscape, of the dawn, of people and animals in harmony to focus on during the time of penitence.
- Lighting the first of the Advent candles (see page 16 for ideas).
- Arrange Old Testament passage to be read by different voices, with some verses by everyone.

Areas of prayer focus around the church

(as described in the 'Open church' days – see page 23)
- Use purple fabric.
- A collection of clocks and watches and calendars, among pictures and headlines of concern, with verses chosen from the day's readings, together with 'Give us grace to cast off the works of darkness and to put on the armour of light' (Collect for the day).

Second Sunday of Advent, Years ABC

Focus of the service:
The whole world waiting in hope. The prophets help us get ready.

Mood:
Hopeful, expectant, listening and attentive.

Possibilities for worship

- Purple streamers and flags.
- Projected images of road building, of people from different cultures, of dawn.
- A font full of water, or several bowls of water around the church, with hand towels, for a time of penitence and affirmation of God's forgiveness. Give people time to come and wash their hands if they would like to.
- Read the Old Testament passage split verse by verse with men and boys, and women and girls.
- Pick a verse or phrase from the day's readings that jumps out at you, to be copied ready for tracing, decorating and displaying. Provide coloured pencils and pens.
- Recorded music from a different area of the world, and a globe prominent as people come into church, with an appropriate text ('Let all the peoples praise him' – Year A; 'Then the glory of the Lord shall be revealed, and all people shall see it together' – Year B; 'All flesh shall see the salvation of God' – Year C).
- Act out the Gospel, in script form, or miming to narration. John the Baptist might be dressed up, even in a token way.
- The second Advent candle is lit.

Areas of prayer focus around the church

- Purple fabric.
- Pictures of people of all ages and cultures crying and being comforted; water with floating candles; globes or world maps.

Phrases to direct people's prayers – 'Pray for better listening', 'Pray for those who don't know God loves them', 'Pray for those who have lost hope' and so on.

Third Sunday of Advent, Years ABC

Focus of the service:
God is coming in person to save us. John the Baptist as the herald.

Mood:
Excitement and joy are building,
as the hope of the kingdom gets closer.

Possibilities for worship

- Purple and silver streamers.
- Projected images of majestic landscapes or skyscapes, of water, of an open gate or door.
- Recorded music which catches the mood of the day.
- Prime different people or groups of people to take part in the Gospel, not coming out together at the front to start with, but shouting from their places, or coming out of their seats as they speak.
- Stage an interview with John the Baptist.
- The third Advent candle is lit.

Areas of prayer focus around the church

- Use both purple and white or gold fabric.
- Phrases to encourage prayers of thanksgiving for God's goodness and loving care; pictures of natural wonders, people's faces; phrases from the readings as encouragement.

Fourth Sunday of Advent, Years ABC

Focus of the service:
The promised kingdom of God's reign will last for ever.
Mary agrees to be part of the plan.

Mood:
Wonder and hope; growing expectation; excitement.

Possibilities for worship

- Purple, pink and silver for streamers, flags and so on.
- The fourth Advent candle is lit. Have someone dressed as Mary to do this, with everyone joining in her words to Gabriel: 'Here I am, the servant of the Lord. Let it be with me as you have said.'
- At different points of the service project images of paintings of the Annunciation from a variety of cultures and times.
- Use paintings or stained glass windows in the church as a focus for the meditation, prayers or talk. (You don't have to agree with the artist's viewpoint – make it a conversation or discussion time.)
- Act out the Gospel reading, with costumes.
- Have a 'Here I am, the servant of the Lord' basket and invite people to write their signature on small pieces of paper and 'sign up to' the statement at the offertory or before the service.

Areas of prayer focus

- Use purple or pink cloths with some silver, to suggest the Advent season being lit by the light of Christmas this week.
- Have a lily with Mary's words at each prayer focus.
- Use pictures and stories from the Christmas charity appeals to highlight needs.
- Print suggestions for prayer: 'Pray for those who are dreading Christmas'; 'Pray that Jesus may be born in our hearts and lives'; 'Pray for those faced with big decisions to make'; 'Pray for the grace to tell others about God's love for us all.'

A parish away-day for Advent:
'Hopes and fears'

Advent is not only an opportunity for outreach to those who don't regularly come to church. It's also an important opportunity for faith nurture and support within the worshipping community. Advent is the start of a new Church year, focused on a different Gospel writer. Year A in the Common Worship Lectionary is broadly focused on Matthew, Year B on Mark and Year C on Luke. (The Gospel of John is used in all three years.) One way of introducing everyone to the Gospel writer of the year is to use an away-day during Advent.

Being the start of the new Church year also places us at a starting point in the yearly liturgical cycle. So it seems sensible to provide space in Advent for the whole community to pray, learn and play their way to a deeper understanding of God's nature and will for us. The 'Last Things' themes of Advent set the scene for all that is to follow, which makes them another possibility for an Advent away-day.

When planning such a day, bear in mind once again that this has become a hectic and stressful time of year for many, and it is not the job of the church to pile on yet more work and stress. A day at this time of year needs to be viewed as a day of inspiration, fun and spiritual refreshment, without any great burdens of preparation or exhausting leadership. Wherever possible, opt for a structure which is self-sustaining and lightweight, so that the whole community views it not with dread but relief.

With all this in mind, I have outlined a choice of two away-days, one following the idea of introducing the current year's Gospel (see page 66), and the other exploring the Advent theme: hopes and fears. Both are designed to work for a mixed-age-group community, and so both are 'hands-on' programmes. They can be adapted easily to your own particular group, and shouldn't take too much organising for any one person.

'Hopes and fears'
Advent explored through art, music, literature and prayer

Suggested timetable

10:00 Welcome, drinks and exhibition

10:30 Opening worship: setting the scene

10:40 Session 1: Art

11:15 Break

11:25 Session 2: Literature

12:00 Bring and share lunch

13:00 Session 3: Music

13:35 Break

13:45 Session 4: Response and discussion

14:30 Closing worship

14:45 Refreshments

15:00 Finish

What you will need . . .

1. A place to meet – perhaps a church hall or school in a different type of location.
2. Facilities for making drinks/soup and washing up.
3. Overhead projector and white wall or screen for projection (or video projector and laptop with PowerPoint).
4. Blank acetates and pens.
5. CD/Tape Player, powerful enough for the size of venue.
6. Flipchart pad and assorted marker pens.
7. Crayons and pencils, paints, scissors, glue and assorted coloured paper, including some shiny paper and foil.
8. Protective plastic sheeting for practical art area.
9. Plenty of tables and chairs.
10. Bibles, some copies of *Common Worship*, and a reading library box.

11. Assortment of percussion instruments and accompaniment for worship if preferred.
12. Copied resource sheets.
13. Willing helpers to set up and clear away.

The exhibition

- Place tables around the walls and bring plenty of cloth to drape over them – bedsheets or curtaining are fine.

- Collect pictures of how artists have expressed their ideas of heaven and hell over the generations. Have art books, owned or borrowed from the library, open at such images, and bookmarks of other pages in them to look at.

- Collect pictures from calendars and nature magazines of the heavenly places on earth.

- Bring symbols of hope, death, judgement, hell and heaven – for example, orange and white candles, a scull and crossed bones 'pirate' flag, a variety of crosses and crucifixes, traditional scales with a feather being weighed, some clanking chain with opened padlock, and a heavy key.

- Choose some of the suggested quotations, questions and Bible references and have these written or printed out among the pictures and symbols.

- Make sure the exhibition is already set up as people come in, and as they are welcomed and given a drink, invite them to browse around the exhibition.

Quotations . . .

Copy and enlarge some or all of the quotations in Appendix 1 on page 71, and display them separately, linked with the pictures and symbols. Add others you find helpful.

And some questions . . .

- Which of these ideas do you agree with? Which do you disagree with?
- How do you think of heaven?
- How do you think of hell?
- As Christians, is it wrong to fear death?
- What do you think the last judgement will be like?
- Where, if anywhere, is heaven?
- Where, if anywhere, is hell?
- What do you think is happening to us at death?
- Where does your hope come from?
- What do you fear about dying?
- Which Bible passages comfort you most?
- Which 'last things' Bible passages worry you?

Opening worship

Include some singing, some praying, a short Bible reading and a short time of quietness in God's presence. Don't make it longer than ten minutes. Have the carpets or rugs down in the centre for the little ones to play on.

Ask for God to put you all in touch with whatever he wants to teach you today as a church community. Pray for the grace to behave lovingly with one another, listening well and looking out for one another's needs.

Session 1: Art

- Beforehand, copy a selection of images of life after death on to acetates, so you can project them using the OHP. (Find these on art image web sites, in art books, and on Christmas cards.) For contrast choose images from different cultures and ages. Have with you any information about who painted the picture, when and where, but don't talk about this yet.

- Arrange everyone in small groups, café style, of mixed ages, with paper and pens for each table group, together with the following questions:
  - What can you see in this picture?
  - What colours are there?
  - How does it make you feel?
  - What is it saying?
- Project one of the images and immediately get everyone talking about their reactions to it, using the guide questions. It's important that there is no introduction, as this will only discourage people from sharing their natural reactions and questions about it. Key points are noted in each group by a scribe. Encourage groups to include all members, giving time for those who take longer to gather their thoughts, and making sure no one hogs the conversation. Questions deliberately cover different levels of looking.
- Follow on with another, contrasting image in the same way. Depending on the group, you may be showing between three and six images.
- Finally project the images in chronological order, with groups calling out any particular observations, likes and dislikes. See which group can get closest to the year the painting was completed and by whom.

Session 2: Literature

- For this session, set up six 'story corners', based on Nursery, Infants, Juniors, Secondary, Lowbrow and Highbrow.
- For each corner have a selection of appropriate literature to listen to or read, and talk about.
- Start by showing a short clip from the Monty Python 'Dead Parrot' sketch, or an appropriate clip from *The Simpsons*.

Nursery

  - Carpeted area with construction toys and modelling activities which involve the satisfaction of completing something.

- Books which are about searching and finding, and being found, like *Where's Spot?*
- Books which are about change and transformation, like *The Very Hungry Caterpillar*.
- Pop-up books which change from two-dimensional pictures to three-dimensional.
- And enough adults to allow for listening and conversation.

Infants

- Carpeted area.
- Story telling or story reading, such as *The Sea of Tranquillity, The Jelly Monster* or *Can't You Sleep, Little Bear?*

Juniors

- Carpeted area.
- Hassocks to sit on.
- Story reading with excerpts from two or three books, such as *Badger's Parting Gifts* or *The Last Battle*, and Voldemort's duel with Harry in *Harry Potter and the Goblet of Fire*.

Secondary

- Carpeted area, chairs and hassocks.
- Reading excerpts from *Sophie's World, River Boy* or something from Terry Pratchett's *Discworld* books.

Lowbrow

- Carpeted area, chairs and hassocks.
- Reading excerpts from Adrian Plass, *Bridget Jones' Diary*, and assorted Nick Hornby or Stephen King novels.

Highbrow

- Carpeted area, chairs and hassocks, bookshelf.
- A library of books with bookmarks at appropriate places for people to browse.
- Opportunity to share favourites with the group.

– Include poetry, such as John Donne, George Herbert, Wilfred Owen, Emily Dickinson, W. B. Yeats, some theology, and novels by Sebastian Faulks, Vikram Seth and Leo Tolstoy.

Session 3: Music

Supply plenty of paper and art materials for those who want to draw and paint what they hear, and play some contrasting excerpts from music inspired by these themes.

Suggestions:

- Dies Irae from Verdi's *Requiem*
- Appropriate film soundtracks
- Benedictus from Gounod's *Requiem*
- Laments and celebrations from around the world

Session 4: Response and discussion

- Each of the small groups of mixed ages have a flipchart sheet of paper titled 'Hopes and fears'. It's divided into four sections by a cross, titled 'Art', 'Music', 'Words', and '???'. Pens and crayons are also provided.
- Discuss and draw or write responses to each section, noting favourites/non-favourites, and how they have changed your thinking about death, judgement, heaven and hell.
- The '???' section is for recording any questions the day has raised about these areas of faith.
- Move around the room looking at other groups' paper and chatting with them.

Closing worship

Display all the finished art and craft, discussion sheets and so on. Have projected the voted favourite of the art images.

Sing together. Suggestions:

- There's a wideness in God's mercy
- The Spirit lives to set us free
- Thine be the glory
- He's got the whole world in his hands
- O, heaven is in my heart
- O Jesus, I have promised
- O come, O come, Emmanuel

Provide streamers and flags and instruments as appropriate.

Prayers of thanksgiving –

either with everyone speaking them out, or by one person voicing everyone's thoughts:

> Lord of the past, the present and the future,
> God of love and mercy,
> we thank you for the gift of this time together.
> We thank you for being here among us now
> and through every moment of our lives,
> through death and on into eternity.
> We worship and adore you!
> Amen.

Have a short 'show and tell' time, when representative people of all ages show artwork or mention any insights given through the day.

Sing again together, and finish with a blessing.

A parish day:
'Gospel writer of the year'

Meet this year's main Gospel writer and his book

The simplest way to do this is to set up the exhibition, refreshments, prayer stations and activities, and have the Gospel read straight through. There are excellent recordings available, some accompanied with sound effects and music, and using different voices.

Or you can stage your own 'read', using good readers and changing the voices regularly. The *Dramatised Bible* will enable you to involve more voices.

Invite people to come and listen, and encourage a relaxed atmosphere which allows them to sit, walk around, get a drink, or respond creatively as they hear the Gospel spoken. The suggestions for the exhibition are on page 67 and for the creative response are on page 68. Prayer stations are explained on page 25.

Begin and end with an act of worship.

Another way of staging this is to have a timetabled programme throughout the day, as follows:

Suggested timetable

10:00 Welcome, drinks and exhibition

10:30 Opening worship: Setting the scene

10:40 Session 1: Hanging out the Gospel line

11:15 Break

11:25 Session 2: Getting the flavour

12:00 Bring and share lunch

13:00 Session 3: Getting creative

13:35 Break

13:45 Session 4: Learning from one another

14:30 Closing worship

14:45 Refreshments

15:00 Finish

The exhibition

- Tables around the walls, draped with fabric in mainly white and purple.
- Copies of the Greek text of the Gospel, open beside a corresponding passage in English.
- A selection of typical phrases used in the style of this particular Gospel writer. Print them out separately, with a Bible reference, so people can see how they form a particular 'voice'.
- Printouts of, or Bibles open at passages only recorded in this Gospel.
- Life and times artefacts such as coins, a 'scroll', pottery, fruit and lighting, and picture history books open at appropriate pages.
- Quotations of what people say about this particular Gospel. A list of books you might like to explore may be found on page 86.

Opening worship

Include some singing, some praying, a short Bible reading and short time of quietness in God's presence. Don't make it longer than ten minutes. Have the carpets or rugs down in the centre for the little ones to play on.

Ask for God to put you all in touch with whatever he wants to teach you today as a church community. Pray for the grace to behave lovingly with one another, listening well and looking out for one another's needs.

Session 1: Hanging out the Gospel line

- Hang up a length of washing line and have ready some pegs.
- In two's or three's, with a Bible for each mixed-age group, flip through the Gospel, calling out key passages. A scribe writes titles for these on cards which the children peg up in order on the line. A piece of coloured cloth separates main sections of the Gospel.
- Colour code the cards with different colours and symbols for teaching, miracles and events.
- Talk through any observations about this general Gospel shape and theme.

Session 2: Getting the flavour

- *A shared read.* Small mixed-age groups each prepare a short passage from the Gospel and then read it to the others, with mimed, visual or musical accompaniment as appropriate.
- *That's typical.* Draw attention to the typical phrases of the Gospel, displayed in the exhibition.
- *Spot the difference.* The small mixed-age groups look at a story or event, which is also recorded in another Gospel. Someone reads the two passages aloud while the others try to spot the differences. On flipchart paper they make a note of any differences, either in content, tone or emphasis.

Session 3: Getting creative

Scroll making

- Have ready two 20cm lengths of dowling (or card tubes from kitchen paper) and a 50cm x 16cm strip of paper for each scroll. (Sizes given are only a guide.)
- Mark the strip of paper into several sections like this:

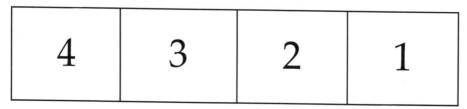

- Starting at the far right side, write or draw your 'page 1'. Work from right to left across the sections for the other pages. Take a Gospel story to draw, or write out.
- Wrap each end of the paper around a stick and fix with sticky tape or glue.
- Roll up your scroll so that the first part you unroll is the far right end. Read it by rolling up from the right and unrolling from the left.

Artwork

- Colour the Gospel writers' symbols on page 87.
- Provide white and coloured paper, pens, pencils, paints and chalks for people to respond freely to the Gospel.

- Have artefacts to draw from life, such as a clay oil lamp, bread and fish, jug of water, lighted candle or pair of sandals.
- Suggest that people take a favourite verse and write it out beautifully, decorating the words. Have some examples of illuminated writing to get them started.
- Provide self-hardening clay and invite people to shape an oil lamp, or roll it into a flat tile and carve a Gospel picture on it.

Greek

- Have the Greek alphabet written out, together with its sounds, so people can have a go at writing their own name in Greek characters. Or they can try saying and writing key words taken directly from the Gospel.
- Have a Diaglott available, or copies of a familiar Gospel passage in word-for-word translation, so people can have a go at turning it into working English.

Drama

- Have simple costumes and props, and scripts taken from the *Dramatised Bible* (or a DIY version).
- Try acting the passage out, and then talking together about any insights gained from actually 'taking part'.
- If this Gospel were a human sculpture, what would it look like and how would it move?

Session 4: Learning from one another

- Spread out all the artwork, poetry, Greek attempts and scrolls for everyone to look at and share. Invite people to share any insights this work has given them.
- Perform the drama/mime.
- In small, mixed-age groups of two's or three's, find out what the others in the group have found out today, and what is their favourite bit of the Gospel.

Closing worship

Keep it short and simple and thankful, and include singing together, with instruments and streamers available. Finish with sharing the Peace and holding hands for the Grace.

Suggestions for singing:

- We have a gospel to proclaim
- God's Spirit is in my heart
- I believe in Jesus
- We'll walk the land
- The Spirit lives to set us free

Appendix 1

I am going now to prepare a place for you, and after I have gone and prepared you a place, I shall return to take you with me; so that where I am you may be too.

John 14:2-4

For the Lamb in the midst of the throne will be their shepherd, and he will guide them to springs of living water; and God will wipe away every tear from their eyes.

Revelation 7:17

Father of Jesus, Love's reward,
what rapture will it be
prostrate before thy throne to lie
and gaze and gaze on thee.

In the end we shall be judged on love; by love we shall be condemned or justified.

Teilhard de Chardin

We are sorting ourselves out now. What comes in the future will only disclose what we have already become.

Mark Gibbard

Give rest, O Christ, to thy servant with thy saints;
where sorrow and pain are no more,
neither sighing, but life everlasting.

The Russian Kontakion

In the evening of life we shall be judged on love alone.

St John of the Cross

God's mercy is my only merit.

Pope John XXIII

Being in heaven is like being in the ocean of God's love and sinking ever deeper for it has no bottom.

I am the resurrection and I am life; he who believes in me, though he die, yet shall he live, and whoever lives and believes in me shall never die.

John 11:25-26

When the Son of Man comes in his glory, and all the angels with him, then he will sit on his glorious throne. Before him will be gathered all the nations, and he will separate them one from another as a shepherd separates the sheep from the goats.

Matthew 25:31-33

Love transforms us slowly into God.
Carlo Carretto

There shall we rest, and we shall see; we shall see and we shall love; we shall love and we shall praise. Behold what shall be in the end and shall not end.

St Augustine

God will show us the path of life; in his presence is the fullness of joy: and at his right hand there is pleasure for evermore.

Psalm 16:11

I am free. The possibility is there that, in face of all that the love of God does to win me through the years, I may yet persist to the last in choosing self-love and in calling white black, and in creating for myself the final isolation. That is hell. It is the self-chosen loneliness of the man or woman who prefers this to the love of God.

Michael Ramsey

For in the last resort there are only two alternatives: either to have God, and in him everything, or to have nothing but yourself. The latter alternative is what Christian theology knows as hell, the former is heaven.

Eric Mascall

For the Christian, all those partial, broken and fleeting perfections which he glimpses in the world around him, which wither in his grasp and are snatched from him even while they wither, are found again, perfect, complete and lasting in the absolute beauty of God, with whom there is no variableness, neither shadow of turning.

Eric Mascall

…And fit us for heaven to live with thee there.
William James Kirkpatrick

Sunday February 9th

That monk who came at Christmas was in church again today. Edwin had asked him to do a question and answer session. Put my fruit-gums away unopened. Father John looked pale and tired, but I honestly thought they'd rigged a spotlight up at the back because there seemed to be a sort of shininess round his face as he sat quietly on a stool at the front.

Mrs Flushpool asked the first question.

She said, 'I find it strange, reverend – I cannot call you Father as I have scriptural reservations – that on your previous visit you barely mentioned the judgement of God on sin committed in the natural. Perhaps you do not feel sinful?'

Father John blinked. 'Oh, I'm a ratbag,' he declared with enthusiasm, 'but I do feel so very forgiven. You see, God's crazy about me, just as he's crazy about you. Salvation was his idea, you know – not ours.' He pointed at Mrs Flushpool. 'If you were to commit a foul sin with every person in your street, and then you said to God, "I really am honestly and sincerely sorry," he would say, "Great! Let's start all over again." Marvellous, isn't it?'

Mrs Flushpool, presumably wrestling inwardly with the image of herself committing foul sins with every person in her street, splashed back down in her seat, looking rather breathless.

Leonard Thynn leaned across and whispered in my ear, 'He knows a different God to the one I do. His God's nice!'

Suddenly I found myself on my feet. Felt about six years old as I spoke.

'I don't want to die . . .'

'No,' said Father John, 'neither do I. Life can be very good. I'm sure Jesus didn't want to die either. His friends and family, the natural world, laughter, tears, work – he loved it all I'm sure.'

'But heaven – the idea of heaven seems so . . . I don't know . . .'

'What is your name?' asked the monk.

'Adrian . . .'

'Adrian, what are you interested in – really interested in, I mean?'

'Cricket.' Didn't mean to tell the truth. It just slipped out.

'So,' said Father John, 'for you, Adrian, God has to make sure that heaven is at least as exciting and stimulating and satisfying as scoring a century against Australia at Lords. Is that your wife sitting next to you?'

Anne smiled and nodded.

'If Adrian keels over suddenly, my dear, and he's on the point of death, you'll know what to do now?'

'Yes,' laughed Anne, 'I'll buckle a pair of pads on him – quick.'

Felt as if someone had opened a window and let air into a stuffy room. Went home for a very enjoyable lunch. I invited Leonard who brought three bottles of wine! Anne and I, knowing poor old Leonard's problems in this area, drank as much of it as we could before he could get his hands on it. Leonard stayed sober, Anne seemed unaffected, but I ended up in the same position as the football team that Gerald supports – struggling at the foot of the table . . .

The Sacred Diary of Adrian Plass

Are limbs, so dear-achieved, are sides,
Full-nerved – still warm – too hard to stir?
Was it for this the clay grew tall?
O what made fatuous sunbeams toil
To break earth's sleep at all?

Wilfred Owen

Here lies one FOOTE, whose death may thousands save,
For death has now one FOOTE within the grave.

Anon

For God himself enters Death's Door always with those that enter
And lays down in the Grave with them, in Visions of Eternity,
Till they awake and see Jesus and the Linen Clothes lying
That the Females had Woven for them, and the Gates of their Father's House.

William Blake

When the day that he must go hence was come, many accompanied him to the river side, into which as he went he said, Death, where is thy sting? And as he went down deeper, he said, Grave, where is thy victory? So he passed over, and all the trumpets sounded for him on the other side.

John Bunyan, 'The Summons of Mr Valiant' from Pilgrim's Progress

Death is the supreme festival on the way to freedom.
Dietrich Bonhoeffer

One short sleep past, we wake eternally,
and Death shall be no more. Death, thou shalt die.
John Donne

There was a time when we were not. This gives us no concern – why then should it trouble us that a time will come when we shall cease to be?
Willam Hazlitt

Dust thou art and unto dust thou shalt return.
Genesis 3:19

Death is but crossing the world, as friends do the sea; they live in one another still.
William Penn

The mind is its own place, and in itself
Can make a heaven of hell, a hell of heaven.

John Milton

There is a dreadful Hell,
and everlasting pains; there sinners must with devils
 dwell
in darkness, fire and chains.

Isaac Watts, Divine Songs for Children

Over the last two centuries . . . there has been the moral protest from both within and without the Christian faith against a religion of fear, and a growing sense that the picture of a God who consigned millions to eternal torment was far removed from the revelation of God's love in Christ. Nevertheless it is our conviction that the reality of hell (and indeed of heaven) is the ultimate affirmation of the reality of human freedom. Hell is not eternal torment, but it is the final and irrevocable choosing of that which is opposed to God so completely and so absolutely that the only end is total non-being. Dante placed at the bottom of hell three figures frozen in ice – Judas, Brutus and Cassius. They were the betrayers of their friends, and through that they had ceased to have the capacity for love and so for heaven. Annihilation might be a truer picture of damnation than any of the traditional images of the hell of eternal torment. If God has created us with the will to choose, then those who make such a final choice choose against the only source of life, and they have their reward. Whether there be any who do so choose, only God knows.

The Mystery of Salvation, p. 199 (The Doctrine Commission of the Church of England)

The New Testament envisages a world enhanced, made more joyful, by the removal of evil. Creation will be free to be itself at last, and we with it. In particular, death, the shadow that falls across all our dreams, will be abolished. The question of whether death was part of God's original creation or whether it, too, is an intruder is a difficult one. Maybe God's original design, that creatures would sleep at the end of their labour, has been changed, because of rebellion, into a threat. Darkness, part of the original creation, has become a symbol of creation's malaise. What was once, perhaps, a kind and wise friend is now a malignant enemy. The promise that death will be abolished assures us both that God will be true to creation and that all our present griefs will at last be healed.

The Meaning of Jesus, p. 199, Tom Wright

But the day of the Lord will come like a thief, and then the heavens will pass away with a loud noise, and the elements will be dissolved with fire, and the earth and everything that is done on it will be disclosed.

2 Peter 3:10

One of the greatest biblical images for God's future is the approaching birth of a baby. It is a time of great hope and new possibility, and also, especially before modern medicine, a time of great danger and anxiety . . . It's only with images like this that one can speak of God's future. We don't have an exact description of it, and we wouldn't be able to cope if we did. What we have are pictures: the birth of a baby, the marriage of a king's son, a tree sprouting new leaves. God's future will be like all these, and (of course) unlike them as well.

Matthew for Everyone, p. 113, Tom Wright

The theme of a last judgement in the New Testament makes the point that how we act within history does matter. Matthew does this in a particularly arresting way with his parable of the sheep and goats . . . What is striking is the criterion by which the judgement is made: have you fed the hungry, welcomed the stranger, clothed the naked, cared for the sick, visited the prisoners? The point of the parable is clear: the most important ethical issue is, 'Have we lived compassionately?'

The Meaning of Jesus, p. 195, Marcus Borg

Bread, forgiveness and deliverance are, of course, always going to be needed as long as the present world continues. But there will come a time when those needs are swallowed up in the complete life of the new age: when God's will is done on earth as in heaven, because heaven and earth have been joined together in the new creation; when God's kingdom, established by Jesus in his death and resurrection, has finally conquered all its enemies by the power of the divine love; and when . . . the name of God is hallowed, exalted and celebrated throughout the whole creation. Every time we say the words 'Our Father . . .' we are pleading for that day to be soon, and pledging ourselves to work to bring it closer.

Matthew for Everyone, p. 210, Tom Wright

In my Father's house there are many dwelling places. If it were not so, would I have told you that I go to prepare a place for you? And if I prepare a place for you, I will come again and will take you to myself, so that where I am, there you may be also.

John 14:2-3

Listen, I will tell you a mystery! We will not all die, but we will all be changed, in a moment, in the twinkling of an eye, at the last trumpet. For the trumpet will sound, and the dead will be raised imperishable, and we will be changed. For this perishable body must put on imperishablity, and this mortal body must put on immortality . . . Then the saying that is written will be fulfilled:

'Death has been swallowed up in victory. Where, O death, is your victory? Where, O death, is your sting?'

1 Corinthians 15:51-55

But filled with the Holy Spirit, Stephen gazed into heaven and saw the glory of God and Jesus standing at the right hand of God. 'Look,' he said, 'I see the heavens opened and the Son of Man standing at the right hand of God!'

Acts 7:55-56

This is indeed the will of my Father, that all who see the Son and believe in him may have eternal life; and I will raise them up on the last day.

John 6:40

I tell you, my friends, do not fear those who kill the body, and after that can do nothing more. But I warn you whom to fear: fear him who, after he has killed, has authority to cast into hell. Yes, I tell you, fear him! Are not five sparrows sold for two pennies? Yet not one of them is forgotten in God's sight. But even the hairs of your head are all counted. Do not be afraid; you are of more value than many sparrows.

Luke 12:4-7

In the resurrection they neither marry nor are given in marriage, but are like angels in heaven. And as for the resurrection of the dead, have you not read what was said to you by God, 'I am the God of Abraham, the God of Isaac, and the God of Jacob'? He is God not of the dead, but of the living.

Matthew 22:30-32

Appendix 2

Book suggestions

Many 'study bibles' have useful introductions to the gospels, and there are many good general Bible commentaries which will include information on each gospel. Here are just a few suggestions:

Richard A. Burridge. *Four Gospels, one Jesus?* (SPCK) 1994

Crossway Bible Guides (SPCK)

Drane, John. *Introducing the New Testament* (Lion)

Green, Joel. *The International Commentary on the New Testament* (Eerdmans) 1997

The International Bible Commentary (SPCK)

Peake's Commentary on the Bible (SPCK)

Wenham and Walton. *Exploring the New Testament. Volume 1: Introducing the Gospels and Acts* (SPCK) 2001

Wright, Tom. *Matthew for everyone (Parts 1 & 2)* (SPCK) 2002

Wright, Tom. *Mark for everyone* (SPCK) 2001

Wright, Tom. *Luke for everyone* (SPCK) 2001

Wright, Tom. *John for everyone (Parts 1 & 2)* (SPCK) 2002

Gospel writers

Acknowledgements

The publishers are grateful to the following for permission to reproduce their copyright material:

SPCK, Holy Trinity Church, Marylebone Rd, London, NW1 4DU, for the quote from *The Meaning of Jesus* by N. T. Wright and M. J. Borg (SPCK 1999), © N. T. Wright and M. J. Borg.

Also for the quote from *Matthew for Everyone* by N. T. Wright (SPCK, 2002), © N. T. Wright. Reproduced by kind permission of the publisher.

The Church of England Archbishops' Council for the quote from *The Mystery of Salvation: The Story of God's Gift* – A report by the Doctrine Commission of the General Synod of the Church of England (Church House Publishing, 1995), © The Archbishops' Council of the Church of England.

Zondervan, 5300 Patterson SE, Grand Rapids, MI 49530, USA, for the quote from *The Sacred Diary of Adrian Plass Aged 37¾* by Adrian Plass (Zondervan, 1990). Copyright © 1987 Adrian Plass. Used by permission.

Every effort has been made to trace the owners of copyright material and it is hoped that no copyright has been infringed. Pardon is sought and apology made if the contrary be the case and a correction will be made in any reprint of this book.